Hamilton Beach Slow Cooker Cookbook

365 Days of Easy Cooking Meals for Any Occasion, Super Delicious Slow Cooker Recipes for Beginners.

D1523426

Abapu Dilande

Table of Contents

INTRODUCTION

The slow cooker is one of the healthy cooking appliances that prepare your food for a longer time at low temperatures. It brings out flavors in food without losing its nutritional value. It is capable of doing all cooking operations smoothly without compromising the taste and texture of the food.

In this cookbook, we have used amazing slow cooker design and manufacture by Hamilton Beach to make your cooking process effortless.

The book contains healthy and delicious slow cooker recipes from breakfast to desserts. All the recipes are done in a Hamilton Beach slow cooker. The recipes written in this book are simple and written in an easily understandable form. The recipes start with their preparation and cooking time with the step of the instruction set. All the recipes written in this cookbook come with their nutritional values which will help you to keep track of daily calorie consumption. I hope you love and enjoy all the slow cooker recipes written in this cookbook.

Chapter 1: Hamilton Beach Slow Cooker

Why Should Go with a Slow Cooker?

The slow cooker is also known as a crockpot which is one kind of countertop electrical appliance equipped with the healthiest cooking functions. There are so many reasons to go with a slow cooker some of them are mentioned as follows.

1.   Healthy cooking appliances:

The slow cooker is one of the healthy cooking appliances because it rarely requires fats and oils during the cooking process. In standard cooking methods, most of the essential vitamins and nutrients are destroyed due to high heat. The slow cooker cooks your food at a very low temperature for a longer period. It simmers your food into its liquid and juices. This helps to preserve the vitamin and nutrients that remain in the food and also enhance the taste of the food.

2.   Quick and easy to use

The slow cooker cooks your favorite food by just putting your ingredients into a crockpot. Then select the desired temperature and time settings as per your recipe needs. Setting low heat settings can take up to 8 hours to cook your food. High settings allow 3 to 4 hours to cook your food perfectly. The slow cooker never overcooks or burns your food. If you are busy or do not want to spend too much time in the kitchen then the Hamilton Beach slow cooker is one of the best appliances available for you.

3.   Great for cheap cuts

The slow cooker is one of the best options for cooking cheap cuts like lamb shoulder, beef brisket, chicken thigh, and pork shoulder. Which contains fats and connective tissues that meltdown during the slow cooking process and add rich and robust flavors to your dish.

4.   Flavors

The slow cooker cooks your food in a sealed environment due to this flavors are locked into the pot and never destroyed through the evaporation process. The slow cooker makes your meat tender and adds rich flavors to your sausages.

5.   Never heat your kitchen

The slow cooker cooks your food at a very low temperature, so it never heats your kitchen while cooking your favorite food. It also uses less electricity and saves your energy bill compared with your average cooker.

What is Hamilton Beach Slow Cooker?

The Hamilton Beach programmable slow cooker comes with a stainless steel finish with plastic handles to stay cool when touched. It has a 6-quart cooking capacity which is enough to cook a 4-pound roast or 6 pounds of chicken. It also comes with patented temperature probes to measure the exact internal temperature of the food and display it on the control panel for precise cooking results. It is loaded with a digital display panel and one-touch operating function buttons to make your cooking easy. The temperature control function allows you to change your cooking level according to your food type. You can cook your food by using high, low, or warm settings for up to 14 hours. The clip-tight gasket lid lock helps to reduce the chances of spilling out food during traveling and cooks your food without making a mess. It gives you 3 choices for effortless cooking which includes probe mode, program mode, and manual mode. Is easy to remove both the glass lid and ceramic crock are dishwasher safe. This makes your cleaning process effortless.

Performance

The performance of the Hamilton Beach slow cooker is better when compared with older models. The latest Hamilton Beach slow cooker comes with various operating functions that give you more flexibility while operating the appliances.

1.   Program Mode:

The program mode allows you to set the time as per your recipe needs and select the LOW or HIGH-temperature settings. This function is ideal when you are busy or away when your slow cooker finished cooking. When you're cooking cycle is done the set-and-forget programmable slow cooker automatically shifts it to WARM mode to keep your food warm until you serve it. This is one of the very convenient features.

How to use:

- Press the ON/OFF button to turn the ON slow cooker.
- Press the PROGRAM button. The cooking time LED illuminates.
- Press arrow buttons to set time or to manual mode, and press arrow buttons to select heat settings.
- Press the ENTER button. Heat settings LED to illuminate.
- Press the arrow button to select heat settings.
- Press the ENTER button to start. 3-seconds beep sounds.

2. Manual Mode:

The manual mode allows you to select the settings between low to high temperatures when you don't know the exact temperature settings. Select the temperature and when the food is ready you just need to set the warm mode to keep it warm until you are ready to serve your food.

How to use:

- Press the ON/OFF button to turn the ON slow cooker.
- Press the MANUAL button. The heat settings LED illuminate.
- Press the arrow button to select the heat settings.
- Press the ENTER button to start. 3-seconds beep sounds.

3. Probe Mode:

This cooking mode is ideal for cooking large cuts of your favorite meat like pot roast, whole chicken, and brisket. While using this mode simply insert the temperature probe inside the meat and set the desired temperature. When the internal temperature of the food reaches the set temperature the slow cooker automatically shifts it to warm mode. This model ensures that the cut of meat is tender and nicely done from the inside.

How to use:

- First, insert the probe inside the food and make sure it is not touching the bottom surface of the slow cooker. Insert the probe jack given on the side of the cooker.
- Press the ON/OFF button to turn the ON slow cooker.
- Press the PROBE button. Heat settings LED to illuminate.
- Press the arrow button to select heat settings from LOW or HIGH
- Press the ENTER button. The Desire Temp LED will illuminate.
- Press the arrow button to select the desired temperature settings.

How to Use Slow Cooker?

The slow cooker comes with a user manual always read it before starting the actual cooking process. The following step-by-step guide will help you with how to use your Hamilton Beach slow cooker.

1.   Preparation

Preparation is one of the important steps to save you're cooking time. You just need to chop the ingredients like vegetables, and meats into chunks. Small chunks are better and cook faster compared with big ones. To give nice color over your favorite meat braise it if needed.

2.   Load ingredients into the pot

When placing ingredients into the slow cooker pot make sure root vegetables are placed at the bottom because it takes a longer time to cook and the food placed at the bottom cooks faster. While cooking your favorite meat place it on top with some liquids like broth, stock, water, and wine to avoid food drying out. To get a better cooking result fill the ingredients into the crock pot not more than 1 inch from the rim.

3.   Cooking process

After loading all incidents into the Hamilton Beach slow cooker place the lid. Set the time and temperature settings. Use low-temperature settings if you want to cook food for a longer time. Use high-temperature settings for short cooking time. Use a temperature probe to measure the exact inside temperature of your food. When finishing the cooking process your slow cooker automatically switches on keep warm mode to keep your food warm until you serve it.

4.   Cleaning

The Hamilton Beach slow cooker has a dishwasher-safe glass lid and ceramic crockpot. You can also wash it using soapy water, Do not immerse the main unit into water it contains electrical components that may cause a short circuit.

Care and Cleaning

Cleaning is one of the essential processes that keep your appliances clean and hygienic. It also improves the lifecycle of your appliances. The following step-by-step cleaning instructions will help you to clean your slow cooker.

1. First, unplug the power cord and allow cooling down your appliances at room temperature.

2. Now remove the crockpot by using oven mitts.

3. Wipe out the metal end of the temperature probe with the help of soapy water then rinse and dry.

4. The glass lid and crock lid both are dishwasher safe. Wash it into hot soapy water rinse and dry.

5. Wipe the base of the main unit with the help of a sponge and damp cloth then dry.

6. After cleaning place all the parts in their original position.

While storing your slow cooker do not clip it.

Chapter 2: Breakfast

Bacon Cheese Casserole

Preparation Time: 10 minutes
Cooking Time: 6 hours
Serve:8

Ingredients:

- 32-ounce (about 907g) frozen hash brown potatoes
- 8 ounce (about 226g) cheddar cheese, shredded
- 1 lb (about 453g) bacon, cooked and crumbled
- 1 teaspoon dry mustard
- 1 bell pepper, diced
- 3 green onions, sliced
- Pepper and salt
- 1 cup milk
- 12 eggs

Method:

1. Spray the slow cooker from the inside with cooking spray.
2. Add hash browns, bacon, onions, cheese, and bell peppers into the slow cooker.
3. In a bowl, whisk eggs with mustard, milk, pepper, and salt.
4. Pour egg mixture over hash brown mixture.
5. Cover and cook on low for 6 hours.

Nutritional Value (Amount per Serving):

- Calories: 840
- Fat: 54.6 g
- Carbohydrates: 44.7 g
- Sugar: 4.6 g
- Protein: 41.1 g
- Cholesterol: 340 mg

Peach Steel Cut Oats

Preparation Time: 10 minutes
Cooking Time: 7 hours
Serve:6

Ingredients:

- 1 tablespoon chia seeds
- ½ teaspoon cinnamon
- 1 cup steel-cut oats
- 2 peaches, chopped
- 1 teaspoon vanilla
- ¼ cup half and half
- ¼ cup water
- 2½ cups milk

Method:

1. Spray the slow cooker from the inside with cooking spray.
2. Add oats and remaining ingredients to the slow cooker and mix well.
3. Cover and cook on low for 7 hours.
4. Stir well and serve.

Nutritional Value (Amount per Serving):

- Calories: 161
- Fat: 5.7 g
- Carbohydrates: 21.6 g
- Sugar: 9.5 g
- Protein: 6.7 g
- Cholesterol: 12 mg

Healthy Breakfast Oatmeal

Preparation Time: 10 minutes
Cooking Time: 6 hours
Serve:8

Ingredients:

- ¼ teaspoon kosher salt
- 2 teaspoon cinnamon
- 2 cups steel-cut oats
- ¼ cup brown sugar
- 1 teaspoon vanilla
- ¼ cup maple syrup
- 3 cups almond milk
- 4 cups water

Method:

1. Spray the slow cooker from the inside with cooking spray.
2. Add oats, vanilla, cinnamon, brown sugar, maple syrup, milk, water, and salt into the slow cooker and mix well.
3. Cover the slow cooker with a lid and cook on low for 6 hours.
4. Top with chopped nuts and serve.

Nutritional Value (Amount per Serving):

- Calories: 330
- Fat: 22.8 g
- Carbohydrates: 30.4 g
- Sugar: 13.6 g
- Protein: 4.8 g
- Cholesterol: 0 mg

Mashed Potatoes

Preparation Time: 10 minutes
Cooking Time: 3 hours
Serve:8

Ingredients:

- 10 medium potatoes, peeled and chopped
- 1 tablespoon parsley, chopped
- ½ teaspoon smoked paprika
- 1 tablespoon garlic, minced
- 1½ cups vegetable stock
- Pepper and salt
- ½ cup sour cream
- ½ cup milk
- ⅓ cup butter

Method:

1. Add potatoes, butter, garlic, stock, pepper, and salt into the slow cooker and stir to combine.
2. Cover and cook on high for 3 hours.
3. Mash potatoes using a masher until smooth.
4. Add parsley, paprika, sour cream, and milk, and stir everything well.

Nutritional Value (Amount per Serving):

- Calories: 293
- Fat: 11.3 g
- Carbohydrates: 43.8 g
- Sugar: 3.9 g
- Protein: 5.7 g
- Cholesterol: 28 mg

Potatoes with Peppers and Onions

Preparation Time: 10 minutes
Cooking Time: 4 hours
Serve:8

Ingredients:

- 3 lb (about 1360g) baby potatoes, quartered
- 2 tablespoon butter, diced
- 2 teaspoons smoked paprika
- 1 tablespoon garlic, minced
- 2 tablespoons olive oil
- ½ medium onion, diced
- 2 bell pepper, diced
- Pepper and salt

Method:

1. Spray the slow cooker from the inside with cooking spray.
2. Add potatoes and remaining ingredients into the slow cooker and stir well.
3. Cover and cook on low for 4 hours.
4. Stir well and serve.

Nutritional Value (Amount per Serving):

- Calories: 169
- Fat: 6.7 g
- Carbohydrates: 24.7 g
- Sugar: 1.9 g
- Protein: 4.9 g
- Cholesterol: 8 mg

Sausage Potato Casserole

Preparation Time: 10 minutes
Cooking Time: 6 hours
Serve:6

Ingredients:

- 32 ounce (about 907g) potatoes, peel and dice
- 10.5 ounces (about 297g) can cream of chicken soup
- 14 ounces (about 396g) kielbasa, cut into pieces
- 2½ cups cheddar cheese, shredded
- ½ cup sour cream
- 1 small onion, diced
- Pepper and salt

Method:

1. Add potatoes, onion, 2 cups cheese, and kielbasa into the slow cooker and mix well.
2. In a bowl, mix sour cream, soup, pepper, and salt and pour over the potato mixture.
3. Sprinkle the remaining cheese on top.
4. Cover the slow cooker with a lid and cook on low for 6 hours.

Nutritional Value (Amount per Serving):

- Calories: 537
- Fat: 34.6 g
- Carbohydrates: 32.9 g
- Sugar: 2.9 g
- Protein: 24.5 g
- Cholesterol: 108 mg

Pumpkin Oats

Preparation Time: 10 minutes
Cooking Time: 7 hours
Serve:6

Ingredients:

- 15 ounces (about 425g) can of pumpkin puree
- 1 tablespoon ground cinnamon
- ¼ cup ground flaxseed meal
- 1½ cups steel-cut oats
- ½ teaspoon ground cloves
- ½ teaspoon ground nutmeg
- 1 teaspoon ground ginger
- ½ teaspoon kosher salt
- 1 tablespoon vanilla
- ¼ cup maple syrup
- 2 cups almond milk
- 3 cups water

Method:

1. Spray the slow cooker from the inside with cooking spray.
2. Add oats and remaining ingredients into the slow cooker and stir well.
3. Cover and cook on low for 7 hours.
4. Stir well and serve warm.

Nutritional Value (Amount per Serving):

- Calories: 432
- Fat: 21.7 g
- Carbohydrates: 55.3 g
- Sugar: 21 g
- Protein: 8.1 g
- Cholesterol: 0 mg

Hearty Breakfast Casserole

Preparation Time: 10 minutes
Cooking Time: 3 hours
Serve:6

Ingredients:

- 10.5 ounces (about 297g) cream of mushroom soup
- 14 ounce (about 396g) smoked sausage, diced
- 32-ounce (about 907g) hash browns
- 1½ cups cheddar cheese, grated
- ½ teaspoon parsley
- ½ teaspoon thyme
- 1 small onion, diced
- 1 cup milk

Method:

1. Place hash browns, sausage, onion, and 1 cup cheddar cheese into the slow cooker.
2. Pour mushroom soup over hash brown mixture and stir well.
3. Sprinkle the remaining cheese and herbs on top.
4. Cover the slow cooker with a lid and cook on high for 3 hours.
5. Serve hot and enjoy.

Nutritional Value (Amount per Serving):

- Calories: 785
- Fat: 49.3 g
- Carbohydrates: 58.2 g
- Sugar: 5.1 g
- Protein: 26.3 g
- Cholesterol: 89 mg

Blueberry Oatmeal

Preparation Time: 10 minutes
Cooking Time: 6 hours
Serve:4

Ingredients:

- ½ teaspoon cinnamon
- ½ cup fresh blueberries
- 2 cups steel-cut oats
- ¼ cup brown sugar
- 2 cups water
- 2 cups milk

Method:

1. Spray the slow cooker from the inside with cooking spray.
2. Add oats remaining ingredients into the slow cooker and mix well.
3. Cover and cook on low for 6 hours.
4. Top with shredded coconut and serve.

Nutritional Value (Amount per Serving):

- Calories: 262
- Fat: 5.2 g
- Carbohydrates: 45.5 g
- Sugar: 16.5 g
- Protein: 9.5 g
- Cholesterol: 10 mg

Carrot Cake Oatmeal

Preparation Time: 10 minutes
Cooking Time: 4 hours
Serve:8

Ingredients:

- ½ cup heavy whipping cream
- ¼ cup pecans, chopped
- 1 teaspoon cinnamon
- 1 cup steel-cut oats
- 1 teaspoon vanilla
- ½ cup raisins
- 1 cup carrot, grated
- ¼ cup maple syrup
- 2 tablespoon butter
- ¼ teaspoon nutmeg
- 2 teaspoon ginger
- 2 cups milk
- 1 cup water

Method:

1. Spray the slow cooker from the inside with cooking spray.
2. Add all ingredients except pecans into the slow cooker and mix well.
3. Cover and cook on low for 4 hours.
4. Top with pecans and serve.

Nutritional Value (Amount per Serving):

- Calories: 211
- Fat: 10.6 g
- Carbohydrates: 26.5 g
- Sugar: 15 g
- Protein: 4.4 g
- Cholesterol: 23 mg

Cinnamon Roll Casserole

Preparation Time: 10 minutes
Cooking Time: 2 hours 30 minutes
Serve:10

Ingredients:

- 24 ounce (about 680g) can cinnamon rolls, cut into quarters
- 3 tablespoons maple syrup
- 1 teaspoon cinnamon
- 2 teaspoons vanilla
- ½ cup milk
- 4 eggs

Method:

1. Spray the slow cooker from the inside with cooking spray.
2. Place cinnamon rolls into the slow cooker.
3. In a small bowl, whisk together eggs, cinnamon, maple syrup, and milk and pour over cinnamon rolls.
4. Cover and cook on low for 2 hours 30 minutes.

Nutritional Value (Amount per Serving):

- Calories: 274
- Fat: 9.7 g
- Carbohydrates: 40.6 g
- Sugar: 19.8 g
- Protein: 5.7 g
- Cholesterol: 66 mg

Flavors Apple Oatmeal

Preparation Time: 10 minutes
Cooking Time: 6 hours
Serve:4

Ingredients:

- 1 tablespoon maple syrup
- 1 cup apple, chopped
- 1 cup steel-cut oats
- 1 teaspoon cinnamon
- 1 teaspoon vanilla
- 2 cups almond milk
- ¼ teaspoon salt
- 2 cups water

Method:

1. Spray the slow cooker from the inside with cooking spray.
2. Add oats and remaining ingredients into the slow cooker and mix well.
3. Cover and cook on low for 6 hours.

Nutritional Value (Amount per Serving):

- Calories: 400
- Fat: 30.1 g
- Carbohydrates: 32.1 g
- Sugar: 13.1 g
- Protein: 5.6 g
- Cholesterol: 0 mg

Cinnamon Raisin Oatmeal

Preparation Time: 10 minutes
Cooking Time: 6 hours
Serve:6

Ingredients:

- 2 teaspoon cinnamon
- ⅛ teaspoon nutmeg
- ⅛ teaspoon cloves
- ½ cup brown sugar
- 1 cup steel-cut oats
- ½ cup raisins
- 2½ cups milk
- 2 cups water

Method:

1. Spray the slow cooker from the inside with cooking spray.
2. Add oats, water, milk, and raisins into the slow cooker and mix well.
3. Cover and cook on low for 6 hours.
4. Stir in nutmeg, cloves, cinnamon, and brown sugar.
5. Stir well and serve.

Nutritional Value (Amount per Serving):

- Calories: 187
- Fat: 3.1 g
- Carbohydrates: 36.3 g
- Sugar: 23.6 g
- Protein: 5.5 g
- Cholesterol: 8 mg

Egg Sausage Mushroom Casserole

Preparation Time: 10 minutes
Cooking Time: 6 hours
Serve:8

Ingredients:

- 13 ounces (about 368g) Italian ground sausage, cooked
- 1½ cups cheddar cheese, shredded
- 2 bell peppers, diced and sautéed
- 2 cups mushrooms, sliced and sautéed
- 2 cups spinach, chopped
- 1 teaspoon garlic powder
- 1 teaspoon onion powder
- 1 teaspoon baking powder
- 1 cup almond flour
- 1 cup milk
- 12 eggs
- ½ teaspoon salt

Method:

1. Spray the slow cooker from the inside with cooking spray.
2. Add sausage, mushrooms, bell peppers, ½ cup cheese, garlic powder, onion powder, baking powder, and salt into the slow cooker and mix well.
3. In a bowl, whisk eggs with spinach, milk, and almond flour and pour over the sausage mixture.
4. Top with remaining cheese.
5. Cover and cook on low for 6 hours.

Nutritional Value (Amount per Serving):

- Calories: 381
- Fat: 28.5 g
- Carbohydrates: 8.6 g
- Sugar: 5 g
- Protein: 24.7 g
- Cholesterol: 299 mg

Tater Tots Casserole

Preparation Time: 10 minutes
Cooking Time: 4 hours
Serve:8

Ingredients:

- 32 ounces (about 907g) frozen tater tots
- 1 cup Colby jack cheese, shredded
- 1 lb (about 453g) ground turkey sausage
- ½ teaspoon garlic powder
- ½ teaspoon dried thyme
- 2 tablespoons heavy cream
- 6 eggs
- Pepper and salt

Method:

1. Spray the slow cooker from the inside with cooking spray.
2. Add tater tots and sausage into the slow cooker.
3. In a bowl, whisk eggs with heavy cream, thyme, garlic powder, pepper, and salt and pour over the tater tots mixture.
4. Cover and cook on low for 4 hours.

Nutritional Value (Amount per Serving):

- Calories: 392
- Fat: 23.5 g
- Carbohydrates: 28.6 g
- Sugar: 1.5 g
- Protein: 168 g
- Cholesterol: 168 mg

Chapter 3: Meat

Lamb Ragu

Preparation Time: 10 minutes
Cooking Time: 8 hours
Serve:8

Ingredients:

- 7 ounces (about 198g) bacon, cooked and crumbled
- 2 lb (about 907g) lamb roast, cut into pieces
- 1.5 lb (about 680g) crushed tomatoes
- 2 tablespoons tomato paste
- 2 teaspoons dried thyme
- 2 teaspoons dried rosemary
- 2 celery stalks, diced
- 2 carrots, diced
- 2 teaspoon garlic, crushed
- 1 cup beef stock
- 2 bay leaves
- 1 onion, diced
- ½ cup red wine

Method:

1. Add lamb roast into the slow cooker.
2. Pour the remaining ingredients over lamb roast.
3. Cover and cook on low for 8 hours. Discard bay leaves.
4. Shred the meat using a fork.
5. Stir well and serve.

Nutritional Value (Amount per Serving):

- Calories: 444
- Fat: 21.4 g
- Carbohydrates: 11.9 g
- Sugar: 6.8 g
- Protein: 40.5 g
- Cholesterol: 119 mg

Beef Potatoes Gratin

Preparation Time: 10 minutes
Cooking Time: 4 hours
Serve:6

Ingredients:

- 3 lb (about 1360g) potatoes, cut into ¼-inch slices
- 3 cups cheddar cheese, shredded
- 1 lb (about 453g) ground beef
- ½ cup chicken broth
- 1 teaspoon parsley
- ½ teaspoon garlic powder
- 1 teaspoon paprika
- 1 cup onion, sliced
- Pepper and salt

Method:

1. Add ground meat, broth, parsley, garlic powder, paprika, onion, pepper, and salt into the slow cooker and mix well.
2. Top with potato slices. Sprinkle shredded cheese on top.
3. Cover and cook on high for 4 hours.

Nutritional Value (Amount per Serving):

- Calories: 537
- Fat: 23.8 g
- Carbohydrates: 38.6 g
- Sugar: 3.9 g
- Protein: 41.5 g
- Cholesterol: 127 mg

Korean Beef

Preparation Time: 10 minutes
Cooking Time: 6 hours
Serve:8

Ingredients:

- 3 lb (about 1360g) chuck roast, cut into 1-inch cubes
- ¼ teaspoon red pepper, crushed
- 1 tablespoon ginger, minced
- 1 tablespoon garlic, minced
- 1 tablespoon sesame oil
- 1 tablespoon canola oil
- ½ cup soy sauce
- 1 cup brown sugar

Method:

1. Place the chuck roast into the slow cooker.
2. Mix oil, brown sugar, soy sauce, sesame oil, garlic, ginger, and red pepper and pour over chuck roast.
3. Cover and cook on low for 6 hours.
4. Stir well and serve.

Nutritional Value (Amount per Serving):

- Calories: 480
- Fat: 17.6 g
- Carbohydrates: 20.1 g
- Sugar: 18.1 g
- Protein: 57.4 g
- Cholesterol: 172 mg

Taco Meat

Preparation Time: 10 minutes
Cooking Time: 4 hours
Serve:8

Ingredients:

- 4 lb (about 1814g) ground beef
- 3 ounces (about 85g) taco seasoning
- 16 ounces (about 453g) jar taco sauce
- ¼ cup chicken stock
- 1½ teaspoon sugar

Method:

1. Add ground beef, sugar, taco seasoning, taco sauce, and stock into the slow cooker and mix well.
2. Cover and cook on high for 4 hours.
3. Stir well and serve.

Nutritional Value (Amount per Serving):

- Calories: 452
- Fat: 15.4 g
- Carbohydrates: 2.4 g
- Sugar: 0.8 g
- Protein: 70.1 g
- Cholesterol: 206 mg

Flavors Beef Steak

Preparation Time: 10 minutes
Cooking Time: 8 hours
Serve:8

Ingredients:

- 2 lb (about 907g) beef round steak, sliced
- 1 teaspoon Worcestershire sauce

- 1½ teaspoon garlic, minced
- ½ teaspoon ground ginger
- 2 tablespoons soy sauce
- 2 bell peppers, sliced
- 1 cup beef broth
- 1 onion, sliced
- Pepper and salt

Method:

1. Place steak into the slow cooker.
2. Pour the remaining ingredients over the steak and mix well.
3. Cover and cook on low for 8 hours.

Nutritional Value (Amount per Serving):

- Calories: 268
- Fat: 10.3 g
- Carbohydrates: 4.3 g
- Sugar: 2.4 g
- Protein: 37.3 g
- Cholesterol: 95 mg

Flavorful Beef Tips

Preparation Time: 10 minutes
Cooking Time: 8 hours
Serve:6

Ingredients:

- 2 lb (about 907g) beef top sirloin steak, cubed
- 1½ tablespoons Worcestershire sauce
- 8 ounce (about 226g) mushrooms, sliced
- 2⅓ cups beef broth
- 1 tablespoon canola oil
- 1 onion, sliced
- Pepper and salt

Method:

1. Add meat, Worcestershire sauce, broth, oil, mushrooms, onion, pepper, and salt into the slow cooker and stir well.
2. Cover and cook on low for 8 hours.
3. Stir well and serve.

Nutritional Value (Amount per Serving):

- Calories: 336
- Fat: 12.4 g
- Carbohydrates: 4.1 g
- Sugar: 2.5 g
- Protein: 49.2 g
- Cholesterol: 135 mg

Hamburger Hash

Preparation Time: 10 minutes
Cooking Time: 8 hours
Serve:8

Ingredients:

- 28 ounces (about 793g) potatoes with onions and peppers, thawed
- 10.5 ounce (about 297g) can onion soup
- 10-ounce (about 283g) cream of mushroom soup
- 15-ounce (about 425g) tomato puree
- 3 lb (about 1360g) ground beef
- 2 cups cheddar cheese, shredded
- 2 cups carrots, diced
- 1 teaspoon salt

Method:

1. Add meat, carrots, potatoes, and salt into the slow cooker and mix well.
2. Mix onion soup, mushroom soup, and tomato puree and pour over the meat mixture.
3. Sprinkle shredded cheese on top.
4. Cover and cook on low for 8 hours.

Nutritional Value (Amount per Serving):

- Calories: 528
- Fat: 21.6 g
- Carbohydrates: 19.1 g
- Sugar: 5.9 g
- Protein: 62.3 g
- Cholesterol: 182 mg

Sausage Casserole

Preparation Time: 10 minutes
Cooking Time: 6 hours
Serve:6

Ingredients:

- 1 tablespoon Worcestershire sauce
- 2 tablespoon butter, melted
- 2 teaspoon garlic, crushed
- 8 Italian sausage, sliced
- 1 teaspoon dried thyme
- 2 tablespoons flour
- 1 onion, chopped
- 1 cup frozen peas
- 1 bay leaf
- 1 carrot, diced
- 3 cups beef stock

Method:

1. Add sausage, onion, carrot, bay leaf, and peas into the slow cooker.
2. Mix butter, garlic, flour, Worcestershire sauce, and stock and pour over the sausage mixture.
3. Cover and cook on low for 6 hours.
4. Stir well and serve.

Nutritional Value (Amount per Serving):

- Calories: 211
- Fat: 14.5 g
- Carbohydrates: 9.5 g
- Sugar: 3 g
- Protein: 10.4 g
- Cholesterol: 40 mg

Mexican Beef

Preparation Time: 10 minutes
Cooking Time: 8 hours
Serve:6

Ingredients:

- 10 ounces (about 283g) of tomatoes with green chilies
- 2½ lb (about 1133g) beef chuck roast
- 1 teaspoon dried oregano
- ½ teaspoon chipotle powder
- ½ teaspoon smoked paprika
- 1 teaspoon garlic powder
- 1½ teaspoon ground cumin
- 1 teaspoon lime juice
- 1 cup beef stock
- 1 jalapeno, sliced
- ½ onion, diced
- Pepper and salt

Method:

1. Place beef chuck roast into the slow cooker.
2. Pour the remaining ingredients over beef chuck roast.
3. Cover and cook on low for 8 hours.
4. Shred the meat using a fork and serve.

Nutritional Value (Amount per Serving):

- Calories: 707
- Fat: 52.9 g
- Carbohydrates: 4.2 g
- Sugar: 0.7 g
- Protein: 50.6 g
- Cholesterol: 195 mg

Healthy Beef and Broccoli

Preparation Time: 10 minutes
Cooking Time: 6 hours
Serve:6

Ingredients:

- 1½ lb (about 680g) beef chuck roast, boneless and sliced
- ½ cup soy sauce, low-sodium
- 3 garlic cloves, minced
- 1 tablespoon sesame oil
- ⅓ cup brown sugar
- 3 cups broccoli florets
- 1 cup beef broth

Method:

1. Add meat, garlic, oil, brown sugar, soy sauce, broccoli florets, and broth into the slow cooker and stir well.
2. Cover and cook on low for 6 hours.
3. Stir well and serve.

Nutritional Value (Amount per Serving):

- Calories: 498
- Fat: 34.2 g
- Carbohydrates: 13.2 g
- Sugar: 9.1 g
- Protein: 33.2 g
- Cholesterol: 117 mg

Chapter 4: Poultry

Flavorful Greek Chicken

Preparation Time: 10 minutes
Cooking Time: 4 hours
Serve:4

Ingredients:

- 14 ounces (about 396g) can tomatoes, diced
- 4 chicken breasts, boneless and skinless
- 2 tablespoons fresh basil, chopped
- ½ teaspoon dried basil
- 2 teaspoons garlic, minced
- 2 tablespoon cornstarch
- ¾ cup milk
- ¾ cup pasta sauce
- ¼ teaspoon pepper
- 1 teaspoon salt

Method:

1. Add pasta sauce and tomatoes into the slow cooker.
2. Whisk together milk and cornstarch and pour into the slow cooker.
3. Stir in dried basil, garlic, pepper, and salt.
4. Add chicken and mix well.
5. Cover and cook on low for 4 hours.
6. Stir in fresh basil and serve.

Nutritional Value (Amount per Serving):

- Calories: 380
- Fat: 13 g
- Carbohydrates: 18 g
- Sugar: 9.6 g
- Protein: 45.6 g
- Cholesterol: 135 mg

Honey Lime Chicken

Preparation Time: 10 minutes
Cooking Time: 4 hours
Serve:6

Ingredients:

- 2 lb (about 907g) chicken breasts, boneless and skinless
- 1 tablespoon garlic, minced
- 2 lime juice
- ¼ cup chicken stock
- ½ cup honey
- ½ teaspoon salt

Method:

1. Place chicken into the slow cooker.
2. Mix honey, stock, lime juice, garlic, and salt and pour over chicken.
3. Cover and cook on low for 4 hours.
4. Shred the chicken using a fork and serve.

Nutritional Value (Amount per Serving):

- Calories: 379
- Fat: 11.2 g
- Carbohydrates: 25 g
- Sugar: 23.5 g
- Protein: 44 g
- Cholesterol: 135 mg

Ranch Chicken

Preparation Time: 10 minutes
Cooking Time: 8 hours
Serve:4

Ingredients:

- 2 lb (about 907g) chicken breasts, boneless and skinless
- 10.5 ounces (about 297g) cream of chicken soup
- 1 ounce (about 28g) ranch seasoning
- 3 tablespoons parmesan cheese, grated
- 4 ounce (about 113g) cream cheese, cubed
- ¼ cup red bell pepper, diced
- ½ cup water

Method:

1. Add chicken to the slow cooker.
2. Pour the remaining ingredients over the chicken.
3. Cover and cook on low for 8 hours.
4. Stir well and serve.

Nutritional Value (Amount per Serving):

- Calories: 650
- Fat: 32.9 g
- Carbohydrates: 7 g
- Sugar: 0.8 g
- Protein: 72.5 g
- Cholesterol: 245 mg

Smothered Chicken

Preparation Time: 10 minutes
Cooking Time: 6 hours
Serve:6

Ingredients:

- 2 lb (about 907g) chicken thighs
- 1 tablespoon Italian seasoning
- 1 cup mushrooms, sliced
- 2 cups kale, sliced
- ¾ cup chicken broth
- ½ cup all-purpose flour
- 1 small onion, sliced
- Pepper and salt

Method:

1. Coat chicken with flour and place it into the slow cooker.
2. Add mushrooms, kale, broth, Italian seasoning, onion, pepper, and salt over chicken.
3. Cover and cook on low for 6 hours.

Nutritional Value (Amount per Serving):

- Calories: 355
- Fat: 12.2 g
- Carbohydrates: 12.1 g
- Sugar: 1 g
- Protein: 46.6 g
- Cholesterol: 136 mg

Savory Chicken Drumsticks

Preparation Time: 10 minutes
Cooking Time: 4 hours
Serve:4

Ingredients:

- 2½ lb (about 1133g) chicken drumsticks
- 2 tablespoons olive oil
- ½ teaspoon onion powder
- 1 teaspoon garlic powder
- 1 teaspoon paprika
- Pepper and salt

Method:

1. Place chicken drumsticks into the slow cooker.
2. Mix oil, onion powder, paprika, garlic powder, pepper, and salt and pour over chicken drumsticks.
3. Cover and cook on low for 4 hours.

Nutritional Value (Amount per Serving):

- Calories: 544
- Fat: 23.3 g
- Carbohydrates: 1.1 g
- Sugar: 0.3 g
- Protein: 78.2 g
- Cholesterol: 249 mg

BBQ Chicken

Preparation Time: 10 minutes
Cooking Time: 6 hours
Serve:8

Ingredients:

- 4 chicken breasts, boneless and skinless
- 2 tablespoons Worcestershire sauce
- 12 ounce (about 340g) BBQ sauce
- ¼ cup brown sugar
- ¾ cup Italian seasoning

Method:

1. Place chicken into the slow cooker.
2. Mix BBQ sauce, Italian seasoning, brown sugar, and Worcestershire sauce and pour over chicken.
3. Cover and cook on low for 6 hours.
4. Shred the chicken using a fork and serve.

Nutritional Value (Amount per Serving):

- Calories: 288
- Fat: 11.8 g
- Carbohydrates: 22.9 g
- Sugar: 18.1 g
- Protein: 21.2 g
- Cholesterol: 80 mg

Chicken with Green Beans and Potatoes

Preparation Time: 10 minutes
Cooking Time: 6 hours
Serve:4

Ingredients:

- 1½ lb (about 680g) baby potatoes, halved
- 1 ounce (about 28g) ranch seasoning
- 2 lb (about 907g) chicken thighs
- 1 lb (about 453g) green beans
- 2 tablespoon garlic, minced
- ½ cup butter, melted

Method:

1. Add chicken, potatoes, and green beans into the slow cooker.
2. In a small bowl, mix butter, garlic, and ranch seasoning and pour over the chicken mixture.
3. Cover and cook on low for 6 hours.

Nutritional Value (Amount per Serving):

- Calories: 797
- Fat: 40.2 g
- Carbohydrates: 30.7 g
- Sugar: 1.7 g
- Protein: 72.6 g
- Cholesterol: 263 mg

Easy Chicken Taco Meat

Preparation Time: 10 minutes
Cooking Time: 4 hours
Serve:12

Ingredients:

- 2 lb (about 907g) chicken breasts, boneless and skinless
- 1 ounce (about 28g) taco seasoning
- ½ teaspoon smoked paprika
- ¼ teaspoon chili powder
- ¼ cup fresh cilantro, chopped
- ⅓ cup butter

Method:

1. Add chicken to the slow cooker.

2. Add butter, taco seasoning, paprika, chili powder, and cilantro on top of the chicken.
3. Cover and cook on low for 4 hours.
4. Shred the chicken using a fork and mix well.

Nutritional Value (Amount per Serving):

- Calories: 195
- Fat: 11 g
- Carbohydrates: 0.5 g
- Sugar: 0 g
- Protein: 22.2 g
- Cholesterol: 82 mg

Honey Mustard Chicken

Preparation Time: 10 minutes
Cooking Time: 6 hours
Serve:4

Ingredients:

- 2 tablespoons Dijon mustard
- 8 chicken thighs, boneless
- ¾ cup chicken stock
- 2 garlic cloves, crushed
- 4 onion spring, sliced
- ¼ cup honey

Method:

1. Place chicken thighs into the slow cooker.
2. Add stock, garlic, onion, mustard, and honey over the chicken.
3. Cover and cook low for 6 hours.
4. Remove chicken from the slow cooker and shred using a fork.
5. Return shredded chicken to the slow cooker.
6. Stir well and serve.

Nutritional Value (Amount per Serving):

- Calories: 633
- Fat: 22.1 g
- Carbohydrates: 19.6 g
- Sugar: 18 g
- Protein: 85.4 g
- Cholesterol: 260 mg

Orange Chicken

Preparation Time: 10 minutes
Cooking Time: 3 hours
Serve:4

Ingredients:

- 1¼ lb (about 566g) chicken breasts, boneless and cut into chunks
- 2 tablespoons green onions, sliced
- 1 tablespoon sesame seeds
- ½ teaspoon garlic, minced
- 1 teaspoon sesame oil
- 1 tablespoon rice vinegar
- ¾ cup orange marmalade
- ¼ cup soy sauce
- ¼ cup vegetable oil
- ¼ cup cornstarch
- Pepper and salt

Method:

1. In a bowl, toss chicken with cornstarch and place it into the slow cooker.
2. Mix vegetable oil, marmalade, soy sauce, vinegar, sesame oil, garlic, pepper, and salt, and pour over chicken and mix well.
3. Cover and cook on low for 3 hours.
4. Garnish with green onions and sesame seeds.

Nutritional Value (Amount per Serving):

- Calories: 603
- Fat: 26.4 g
- Carbohydrates: 49.2 g
- Sugar: 36.4 g
- Protein: 42.7 g
- Cholesterol: 126 mg

Italian Lemon Chicken

Preparation Time: 10 minutes
Cooking Time: 4 hours
Serve:4

Ingredients:

- 4 chicken breasts, boneless and skinless
- 1 lb (about 453g) pasta, cooked and drained
- 1 ounce (about 28g) Italian dressing mix
- 2 tablespoon capers, drained
- 2 garlic cloves, minced
- ½ cup chicken broth
- ¼ cup lemon juice
- ½ cup butter, sliced
- Pepper and salt

Method:

1. Add chicken to the slow cooker.
2. Add garlic, broth, lemon juice, Italian dressing mix, butter, pepper, and salt over chicken.
3. Cover and cook on high for 4 hours.
4. Shred the chicken using a fork.
5. Add capers and stir well.
6. Place cooked pasta on a plate and top with chicken.

Nutritional Value (Amount per Serving):

- Calories: 841
- Fat: 37 g
- Carbohydrates: 67.7 g
- Sugar: 0.5 g
- Protein: 56.5 g
- Cholesterol: 274 mg

Easy Chicken Fajitas

Preparation Time: 10 minutes
Cooking Time: 3 hours
Serve:4

Ingredients:

- 2 lb (about 907g) chicken breasts, boneless and sliced
- 7.5 ounces (about 212g) can tomatoes, diced
- 7.5 ounces (about 212g) can of salsa
- 2 tablespoon fajita seasoning
- 1 red bell pepper, sliced
- 1 yellow bell pepper, sliced
- 1 onion, sliced
- Pepper and salt

Method:

1. Place chicken into the slow cooker.
2. Add fajita seasoning, tomatoes, salsa, onion, bell peppers, pepper, and salt over chicken.
3. Cover and cook on high for 3 hours.
4. Stir well and serve.

Nutritional Value (Amount per Serving):

- Calories: 505
- Fat: 17.1 g
- Carbohydrates: 16.4 g
- Sugar: 6 g
- Protein: 67.4 g
- Cholesterol: 202 mg

Creamy Broccoli Chicken

Preparation Time: 10 minutes
Cooking Time: 6 hours
Serve:6

Ingredients:

- 1½ lb (about 680g) chicken breasts, boneless and diced
- 20-ounce (about 567g) cream of mushroom soup
- 2 cups cheddar cheese, shredded
- 1 small onion, diced
- 6 cups broccoli florets
- 2 cups mushrooms, sliced
- ¼ teaspoon garlic powder
- ¼ teaspoon onion powder
- Pepper and salt

Method:

1. Add chicken to the slow cooker.
2. Pour soup, cheese, onion, broccoli florets, mushrooms, garlic powder, onion powder, pepper, and salt over chicken.
3. Cover and cook on low for 6 hours.
4. Stir well and serve.

Nutritional Value (Amount per Serving):

- Calories: 448
- Fat: 24 g
- Carbohydrates: 11.7 g
- Sugar: 3.4 g
- Protein: 46.4 g
- Cholesterol: 140 mg

Balsamic Chicken

Preparation Time: 10 minutes
Cooking Time: 6 hours
Serve:4

Ingredients:

- 4 chicken breasts, boneless and skinless
- 1 tablespoon garlic, minced
- 2 tablespoons brown sugar
- ⅓ cup balsamic vinegar
- ¼ cup chicken stock

Method:

1. Place chicken breasts into the slow cooker.
2. In a bowl, mix vinegar, sugar, garlic, and stock and pour over chicken.
3. Cover and cook on low for 6 hours.

Nutritional Value (Amount per Serving):

- Calories: 302
- Fat: 10.9 g
- Carbohydrates: 5.3 g
- Sugar: 4.5 g
- Protein: 42.4 g
- Cholesterol: 130 mg

Herbed Chicken

Preparation Time: 10 minutes
Cooking Time: 4 hours
Serve:6

Ingredients:

- 1 tablespoon Italian seasoning
- 3 cups baby potatoes, halved

- 1 teaspoon dried mixed herbs
- 1 teaspoon garlic powder
- 3 tablespoons olive oil
- 6 chicken thighs
- Pepper and salt

Method:

1. Place chicken into the slow cooker and top with garlic powder, Italian seasoning, oil, potatoes, herbs, pepper, and salt and mix well.
2. Cover and cook on low for 4 hours.

Nutritional Value (Amount per Serving):

- Calories: 357
- Fat: 18.5 g
- Carbohydrates: 3 g
- Sugar: 0.3 g
- Protein: 42.8 g
- Cholesterol: 132 mg

Flavorful Chicken Carnitas

Preparation Time: 10 minutes
Cooking Time: 8 hours
Serve:6

Ingredients:

- 5 chicken breasts, boneless and skinless
- 1 ounce (about 28g) taco seasoning
- 2 tablespoon garlic, minced
- 1½ cups chicken stock
- ⅓ cup orange juice
- ⅓ cup lime juice
- 1 cup onion, chopped
- 1 jalapeno, diced

Method:

54

1. Place chicken breasts into the slow cooker and pour the remaining ingredients over the chicken.
2. Cover and cook on low for 8 hours.
3. Shred the chicken using a fork and serve.

Nutritional Value (Amount per Serving):

- Calories: 263
- Fat: 9.8 g
- Carbohydrates: 5.4 g
- Sugar: 2.3 g
- Protein: 36.5 g
- Cholesterol: 110 mg

Asian Chicken Drumsticks

Preparation Time: 10 minutes
Cooking Time: 4 hours
Serve:6

Ingredients:

- 3 lb (about 1360g) chicken drumsticks
- ¼ cup soy sauce, low-sodium
- 1 teaspoon ground ginger
- 1 tablespoon sriracha
- 6 garlic cloves, minced
- 2 tablespoons brown sugar
- ¼ cup balsamic vinegar
- ¼ cup honey

Method:

1. Place chicken drumsticks into the slow cooker.
2. Mix honey, soy sauce, vinegar, sugar, garlic, Sriracha, and ginger pour over chicken drumsticks, and coat well.
3. Cover and cook on low for 4 hours.

Nutritional Value (Amount per Serving):

- Calories: 453
- Fat: 13 g
- Carbohydrates: 17.2 g
- Sugar: 14.8 g
- Protein: 63.3 g
- Cholesterol: 200 mg

Juicy Chicken Legs

Preparation Time: 10 minutes
Cooking Time: 4 hours
Serve:6

Ingredients:

- 3 lb (about 1360g) chicken legs
- 2 teaspoons garlic, minced
- ⅓ cup soy sauce
- ½ cup ketchup
- 1 cup apricot jam

Method:

1. Place chicken legs into the slow cooker.
2. In a small bowl, mix apricot jam, ketchup, soy sauce, and garlic and pour over chicken legs.
3. Cover and cook on high for 4 hours.

Nutritional Value (Amount per Serving):

- Calories: 588
- Fat: 17 g
- Carbohydrates: 40.8 g
- Sugar: 28 g
- Protein: 67.3 g
- Cholesterol: 202 mg

Delicious Chicken and Rice

Preparation Time: 10 minutes
Cooking Time: 6 hours
Serve:6

Ingredients:

- 14 ounce (about 396g) can black beans, drained and rinsed
- 14-ounce (about 396g) can of corn, drained

- 4 chicken breasts, boneless and diced
- 2 cups cheddar cheese, shredded
- 14-ounce (about 396g) can of tomatoes
- 1 tablespoon taco seasoning
- 1 can cream of chicken soup
- 3 cups cooked rice
- 1 teaspoon paprika
- 1 cup milk
- ½ onion, diced
- Pepper and salt

Method:

1. Place chicken into the slow cooker and top with paprika, taco seasoning, milk, tomatoes, soup, black beans, onion, corn, pepper, and salt, and mix well.
2. Cover and cook on low for 6 hours.
3. Stir in cheese and cooked rice.

Nutritional Value (Amount per Serving):

- Calories: 879
- Fat: 25.3 g
- Carbohydrates: 109 g
- Sugar: 7.6 g
- Protein: 53 g
- Cholesterol: 134 mg

Pineapple Chicken

Preparation Time: 10 minutes
Cooking Time: 3 hours
Serve:4

Ingredients:

- 4 chicken thighs, bone-in and skin-on
- 20 ounces (about 567g) of crushed pineapple
- 1 tablespoon Worcestershire sauce
- 1 tablespoon garlic, minced

- ½ cup light brown sugar
- Pepper and salt

Method:

1. Place chicken into the slow cooker and top with garlic, brown sugar, pineapple, Worcestershire sauce, pepper, and salt.
2. Cover and cook on high for 3 hours.
3. Stir well and serve.

Nutritional Value (Amount per Serving):

- Calories: 424
- Fat: 11 g
- Carbohydrates: 37.8 g
- Sugar: 32.3 g
- Protein: 43.2 g
- Cholesterol: 130 mg

Chapter 5: Vegetables

Vegetable Cauliflower Rice

Preparation Time: 10 minutes
Cooking Time: 4 hours 10 minutes
Serve:4

Ingredients:

- 5 cups mixed vegetables, chopped
- 3 cups cauliflower rice
- 2 tablespoons brown sugar
- 6 tablespoons soy sauce
- ¼ cup chili garlic sauce
- 1 celery stick, chopped
- Pepper and salt

Method:

1. Add vegetables, brown sugar, soy sauce, chili garlic sauce, celery, pepper, and salt into the slow cooker and stir well.
2. Cover and cook on low for 4 hours.
3. Stir in cauliflower rice and cook for 10 minutes more.

Nutritional Value (Amount per Serving):

- Calories: 185
- Fat: 2.3 g
- Carbohydrates: 33.5 g
- Sugar: 8 g
- Protein: 8.8 g
- Cholesterol: 0 mg

Parmesan Brussels Sprouts

Preparation Time: 10 minutes
Cooking Time: 3 hours
Serve:6

Ingredients:

- 2 lb (about 907g) Brussels sprouts, trimmed and cut in half
- ¾ cup parmesan cheese, shredded
- 1 tablespoon garlic, chopped
- 2 tablespoon butter
- 2 tablespoons olive oil
- Pepper and salt

Method:

1. Add Brussels sprouts, butter, oil, garlic, pepper, and salt into the slow cooker and stir well.
2. Cover and cook on low for 3 hours.
3. Top with parmesan cheese and serve.

Nutritional Value (Amount per Serving):

- Calories: 176
- Fat: 11.4 g
- Carbohydrates: 14.6 g
- Sugar: 3.3 g
- Protein: 8.8 g
- Cholesterol: 18 mg

Flavors Sweet Potatoes

Preparation Time: 10 minutes
Cooking Time: 3 hours
Serve:6

Ingredients:

- 2½ lb (about 1133g) sweet potatoes, peeled and chopped
- 1 tablespoon coconut oil, melted
- 1 tablespoon pumpkin pie spice
- 1 garlic clove, minced
- ½ cup vegetable broth
- 1 bell pepper, diced
- ⅓ cup onion, diced
- Pepper and salt

Method:

1. Add sweet potatoes and remaining ingredients into the slow cooker and stir well.
2. Cover and cook on high for 3 hours.
3. Stir well and serve.

Nutritional Value (Amount per Serving):

- Calories: 259
- Fat: 2.9 g
- Carbohydrates: 55.7 g
- Sugar: 2.4 g
- Protein: 3.6 g
- Cholesterol: 0 mg

Perfect Sweet Carrots

Preparation Time: 10 minutes
Cooking Time: 3 hours
Serve:8

Ingredients:

- 2 lb (about 907g) carrots, peeled and cut into ½-inch pieces
- 1 tablespoon parsley, chopped
- ⅛ teaspoon nutmeg
- ¼ teaspoon cinnamon
- ⅓ cup brown sugar
- ¼ cup butter, melted
- ½ teaspoon salt

Method:

1. Add carrots to the slow cooker.
2. Mix remaining ingredients pour over carrots and mix well.
3. Cover and cook on high for 3 hours.
4. Stir well and serve.

Nutritional Value (Amount per Serving):

- Calories: 121
- Fat: 5.8 g
- Carbohydrates: 17.2 g
- Sugar: 11.5 g
- Protein: 1 g
- Cholesterol: 15 mg

Green Beans with Potatoes

Preparation Time: 10 minutes
Cooking Time: 4 hours
Serve:6

Ingredients:

- 2 lb (about 907g) green beans, trimmed and chopped
- 1 lb (about 453g) baby potatoes, cut in half
- ½ lb (about 226g) bacon, chopped
- 3 cups chicken broth
- 2 garlic cloves, minced
- 1 small onion, sliced
- Pepper and salt

Method:

1. Add green beans and remaining ingredients into the slow cooker and stir well.
2. Cover and cook on high for 4 hours.
3. Stir well and serve.

Nutritional Value (Amount per Serving):

- Calories: 321
- Fat: 16.8 g
- Carbohydrates: 22.6 g
- Sugar: 3 g
- Protein: 21.3 g
- Cholesterol: 42 mg

Chapter 6: Desserts

Delicious Cinnamon Apples

Preparation Time: 10 minutes
Cooking Time: 2 hours
Serve:6

Ingredients:

- 3 lb (about 1360g) apples, peeled and sliced
- 2 tablespoon cornstarch
- 1 teaspoon vanilla
- 2 teaspoons lemon juice
- ¼ cup butter, melted
- 1 teaspoon cinnamon
- ¼ cup sugar
- ¼ cup brown sugar

Method:

1. Spray the slow cooker from the inside with cooking spray.
2. Add apples and remaining ingredients into the slow cooker and stir well.
3. Cover and cook on high for 2 hours.
4. Stir well and serve.

Nutritional Value (Amount per Serving):

- Calories: 194
- Fat: 7.9 g
- Carbohydrates: 32.5 g
- Sugar: 25.9 g
- Protein: 0.4 g
- Cholesterol: 20 mg

Rice Pudding

Preparation Time: 10 minutes
Cooking Time: 2 hours 30 minutes
Serve:4

Ingredients:

- 1.5 ounces (about 42g) butter, unsalted
- ¾ cup long-grain rice
- 1 teaspoon vanilla
- 1 cinnamon stick
- ½ cup sugar
- 4 cups milk

Method:

1. Spray the slow cooker from the inside with cooking spray.
2. Add rice and remaining ingredients into the slow cooker and stir well.
3. Cover and cook on low for 2 hours 30 minutes.
4. Stir well and serve.

Nutritional Value (Amount per Serving):

- Calories: 423
- Fat: 13.9 g
- Carbohydrates: 65.3 g
- Sugar: 36.2 g
- Protein: 10.6 g
- Cholesterol: 43 mg

Blueberry Cobbler

Preparation Time: 10 minutes
Cooking Time: 3 hours
Serve:4

Ingredients:

- 4 cups blueberries
- 8 tablespoon butter, melted
- 1 tablespoon cornstarch
- 3½ teaspoon baking powder
- 1¼ cups granulated sugar
- 2 ¼ cups all-purpose flour

- 1 teaspoon cinnamon
- 1 teaspoon salt

Method:

1. Spray the slow cooker from the inside with cooking spray.
2. Add blueberries to the slow cooker.
3. In a small bowl, mix flour, cinnamon, cornstarch, baking powder, sugar, and salt and sprinkle over blueberries.
4. Drizzle with melted butter.
5. Cover and cook on low for 3 hours.

Nutritional Value (Amount per Serving):

- Calories: 790
- Fat: 24.3 g
- Carbohydrates: 141.5 g
- Sugar: 77.1 g
- Protein: 8.6 g
- Cholesterol: 61 mg

Pineapple Cake

Preparation Time: 10 minutes
Cooking Time: 2 hours
Serve:4

Ingredients:

- 14 ounces (about 396g) can pineapples pieces, drained
- 4 ounce (about 113g) butter, cubed
- 14 ounces (about 396g) yellow cake mix

Method:

1. Add pineapple pieces to the slow cooker.
2. Sprinkle cake mix on top.
3. Spread butter on top. Cover and cook on high for 2 hours.

Nutritional Value (Amount per Serving):

- Calories: 696
- Fat: 34.5 g

- Carbohydrates: 93.6 g
- Sugar: 57.5 g
- Protein: 5.4 g
- Cholesterol: 63 mg

Peach Cobbler

Preparation Time: 10 minutes
Cooking Time: 5 hours
Serve:8

Ingredients:

- 6 cups peaches, sliced and drained
- ⅓ cup buttermilk baking mix
- 1 teaspoon cinnamon
- ½ cup brown sugar
- ⅔ cup quick oats
- ½ cup water

Method:

1. Spray the slow cooker from the inside with cooking spray.
2. Add peaches to the slow cooker.
3. Pour the remaining ingredients on top of peaches.
4. Cover and cook on low for 5 hours.

Nutritional Value (Amount per Serving):

- Calories: 126
- Fat: 1.5 g
- Carbohydrates: 27.3 g
- Sugar: 19.9 g
- Protein: 2.4 g
- Cholesterol: 0 mg

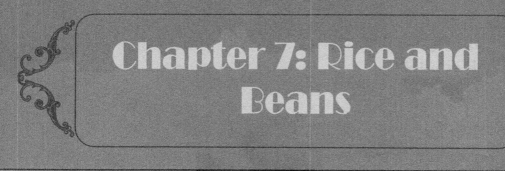

Chapter 7: Rice and Beans

Red Beans with Sausage

Preparation Time: 10 minutes
Cooking Time: 6 hours
Serve:8

Ingredients:

- 1 lb (about 453g) dried red beans, soaked overnight and drained
- 1 lb (about 453g) smoked sausage, sliced
- 2 tablespoon Creole seasoning
- 3 cups chicken broth
- 4 cups water
- 3 garlic cloves, minced
- 1 small onion, diced
- 1 bell pepper, diced

Method:

1. Add beans, sausage, and remaining ingredients into the slow cooker and stir well.
2. Cover and cook on high for 6 hours.
3. Stir well and serve.

Nutritional Value (Amount per Serving):

- Calories: 408
- Fat: 17.3 g
- Carbohydrates: 37.4 g
- Sugar: 2.6 g
- Protein: 25.9 g
- Cholesterol: 48 mg

Spicy Pinto Beans

Preparation Time: 10 minutes
Cooking Time: 8 hours
Serve:6

Ingredients:

- 1 lb (about 453g) pinto beans, soaked overnight and drained
- 15 ounces (about 425g) can of tomatoes, diced
- 14 ounces (about 396g) beef broth
- 32 ounces (about 907g) vegetable broth
- 8 bacon slices, cooked and crumbled
- 2 jalapenos, chopped
- 1 teaspoon cumin
- 1 teaspoon garlic powder
- 1 tablespoon garlic, minced
- 1 medium onion, sliced
- Pepper and salt

Method:

1. Add beans and remaining ingredients into the slow cooker and stir everything well.
2. Cover and cook on high for 8 hours.
3. Stir well and serve.

Nutritional Value (Amount per Serving):

- Calories: 463
- Fat: 12.9 g
- Carbohydrates: 55 g
- Sugar: 5.7 g
- Protein: 31.1 g
- Cholesterol: 28 mg

Black Bean Chili

Preparation Time: 10 minutes
Cooking Time: 8 hours
Serve:6

Ingredients:

- 1 lb (about 453g) black beans, dried and rinsed
- 3 ounces (about 85g) of tomato paste

- 30 ounces (about 850g) tomatoes, diced
- ½ teaspoon baking soda
- 2 tablespoons chili powder
- ½ teaspoon garlic powder
- 1 teaspoon cumin
- 2¾ cups water
- 1 onion, chopped
- ½ teaspoon salt

Method:

1. Add black beans and remaining ingredients into the slow cooker and stir well.
2. Cover and cook on low for 8 hours.
3. Stir well and serve.

Nutritional Value (Amount per Serving):

- Calories: 312
- Fat: 1.9 g
- Carbohydrates: 58.7 g
- Sugar: 8.1 g
- Protein: 18.8 g
- Cholesterol: 0 mg

Herbed Brown Rice

Preparation Time: 10 minutes
Cooking Time: 3 hours
Serve:4

Ingredients:

- 8 ounce (about 226g) mushrooms, sliced
- ½ teaspoon dried oregano
- ½ teaspoon dried thyme
- 4 cups chicken broth
- 2 tablespoon butter, melted
- 2 cups brown rice
- Pepper and salt

Method:

1. Add brown rice, oregano, thyme, broth, mushrooms, butter, pepper, and salt into the slow cooker and mix well.
2. Cover and cook on high for 3 hours.
3. Stir well and serve.

Nutritional Value (Amount per Serving):

- Calories: 446
- Fat: 9.9 g
- Carbohydrates: 75.4 g
- Sugar: 1.7 g
- Protein: 13.9 g
- Cholesterol: 15 mg

Spanish Rice

Preparation Time: 10 minutes
Cooking Time: 3 hours
Serve:12

Ingredients:

- 14 ounces (about 396g) can tomatoes, diced
- 2 tablespoons cilantro, chopped
- 1½ teaspoon ground cumin
- 2 teaspoon chili powder
- 2 bell peppers, diced
- 1½ teaspoon garlic, minced
- 2 cups white rice
- 2 cups tomato sauce
- 2 cups chicken broth
- 1 onion, diced
- 2 tablespoons olive oil
- 1½ teaspoon salt

Method:

1. Add rice and remaining ingredients into the slow cooker and

mix well.

2. Cover and cook on high for 3 hours.
3. Stir well and serve.

Nutritional Value (Amount per Serving):

- Calories: 169
- Fat: 3 g
- Carbohydrates: 31.5 g
- Sugar: 4.5 g
- Protein: 4.3 g
- Cholesterol: 0 mg

Mexican Beans

Preparation Time: 10 minutes
Cooking Time: 12 hours
Serve:10

Ingredients:

- 1 lb (about 453g) pinto beans, rinsed and drained
- 6 bacon slices, cooked and diced
- 1 tablespoon garlic, minced
- 1 tablespoon tomato paste
- ½ cup onion, diced
- 2 jalapenos, sliced
- 6 cups water
- 1 cup salsa
- 1 teaspoon salt

Method:

1. Add pinto beans and remaining ingredients into the slow cooker and stir well.
2. Cover and cook on low for 12 hours.
3. Stir well and serve.

Nutritional Value (Amount per Serving):

- Calories: 232
- Fat: 5.4 g
- Carbohydrates: 31.5 g
- Sugar: 2.3 g
- Protein: 14.6 g
- Cholesterol: 13 mg

Chicken Rice

Preparation Time: 10 minutes
Cooking Time: 6 hours
Serve:8

Ingredients:

- 1½ lb (about 680g) chicken breasts, boneless and diced
- 12 ounce (about 340g) frozen peas and carrots
- 2 cups long-grain rice, uncooked
- 2 cups cheddar cheese, shredded
- 3 cups chicken broth
- 1 can cream of chicken soup

Method:

1. Place chicken and remaining ingredients into the slow cooker and mix well.
2. Cover and cook on low for 6 hours.
3. Stir well and serve.

Nutritional Value (Amount per Serving):

- Calories: 513
- Fat: 18.9 g
- Carbohydrates: 44.7 g
- Sugar: 2.5 g
- Protein: 39 g
- Cholesterol: 108 mg

Black Bean Rice

Preparation Time: 10 minutes
Cooking Time: 3 hours
Serve:6

Ingredients:

- 28 ounce (about 793g) can black beans, rinsed and drained

- 1 teaspoon lime zest
- ¼ teaspoon chili powder
- 1 teaspoon onion powder
- 1 teaspoon garlic powder
- 1 teaspoon taco seasoning
- 1¼ cups vegetable broth
- 1 teaspoon cumin
- 1 cup salsa
- 1 cup Arborio rice
- ¼ teaspoon salt

Method:

1. Add beans, chili powder, onion powder, garlic powder, taco seasoning, cumin, salsa, broth, rice, and salt into the slow cooker and stir well.
2. Cover and cook on low for 3 hours.
3. Stir in lime zest and serve.

Nutritional Value (Amount per Serving):

- Calories: 264
- Fat: 1.3 g
- Carbohydrates: 52.7 g
- Sugar: 2.8 g
- Protein: 11.3 g
- Cholesterol: 1 mg

Mushroom Rice

Preparation Time: 10 minutes
Cooking Time: 2 hours
Serve: 8

Ingredients:

- 1 lb (about 453g) mushrooms, sliced and sautéed
- 3 tablespoon butter, melted
- 1 onion, diced and sautéed
- ½ teaspoon dried thyme
- 2 garlic cloves, minced
- 4 cups beef broth
- 2 cups rice
- Pepper and salt

Method:

1. Add butter, rice, and remaining ingredients into the slow cooker and mix well.

2. Cover and cook on high for 2 hours.
3. Stir well and serve.

Nutritional Value (Amount per Serving):

- Calories: 245
- Fat: 5.5 g
- Carbohydrates: 40.9 g
- Sugar: 2 g
- Protein: 7.8 g
- Cholesterol: 11 mg

BBQ Beans

Preparation Time: 10 minutes
Cooking Time: 4 hours
Serve:8

Ingredients:

- 1 lb (about 453g) ground beef, browned
- 15 ounces (about 425g) pork and beans, un-drained
- 15 ounces (about 425g) red beans, un-drained
- 15 ounce (about 425g) lima beans, un-drained
- 8 bacon slices, cooked and crumbled
- ¼ cup brown sugar
- ¼ cup sugar
- ½ cup BBQ sauce

Method:

1. Add meat and remaining ingredients into the slow cooker and stir everything well.
2. Cover and cook on low for 4 hours.
3. Stir well and serve.

Nutritional Value (Amount per Serving):

- Calories: 564
- Fat: 12.9 g
- Carbohydrates: 69.7 g
- Sugar: 18.1 g
- Protein: 42.9 g
- Cholesterol: 72 mg

Chapter 8: Soup and Stew

Tomato Curried Soup

Preparation Time: 10 minutes
Cooking Time: 4 hours
Serve:8

Ingredients:

- 4 lb (about 1814g) tomatoes, cored and diced
- 2 tablespoon onion, minced
- 1 teaspoon garlic, minced
- 2 teaspoon curry powder
- 2 cups coconut milk
- 1 cup water
- 1 teaspoon salt

Method:

1. Add tomatoes and remaining ingredients into the slow cooker and stir well.
2. Cover and cook on high for 4 hours.
3. Puree the soup using a blender until smooth.
4. Stir well and serve.

Nutritional Value (Amount per Serving):

- Calories: 182
- Fat: 14.8 g
- Carbohydrates: 12.8 g
- Sugar: 8.1 g
- Protein: 3.5 g
- Cholesterol: 0 mg

Southwestern Soup

Preparation Time: 10 minutes
Cooking Time: 6 hours
Serve:2

Ingredients:

- 4 ounces (about 113g) can tomatoes, crushed
- 14 ounces (about 396g) vegetable broth
- ½ tablespoon Worcestershire sauce
- ¼ cup carrots, sliced
- 1 garlic clove, minced
- ½ cup potatoes, diced
- ¼ cup onion, diced

Method:

1. Add tomatoes and remaining ingredients into the slow cooker and stir well.
2. Cover and cook on low for 6 hours.
3. Stir well and serve.

Nutritional Value (Amount per Serving):

- Calories: 87
- Fat: 1.2 g
- Carbohydrates: 13.5 g
- Sugar: 5 g
- Protein: 5.5 g
- Cholesterol: 0 mg

Asparagus Cauliflower Soup

Preparation Time: 10 minutes
Cooking Time: 6 hours
Serve:2

Ingredients:

- 1 lb (about 453g) asparagus, cut into ½-inch pieces
- 1 large onion, chopped and sauteed
- 1 cup cauliflower, chopped
- 2 tablespoons olive oil
- 3 cups vegetable broth
- 1 lemon juice

- Pepper and salt

1. Add asparagus and remaining ingredients into the slow cooker and stir well.
2. Cover and cook on low for 6 hours.
3. Puree the soup using a blender until smooth.
4. Season soup with pepper and salt.
5. Stir well and serve.

Nutritional Value (Amount per Serving):

- Calories: 45
- Fat: 2.8 g
- Carbohydrates: 3.4 g
- Sugar: 1.7 g
- Protein: 2.4 g
- Cholesterol: 0 mg

Vegetable Bean Soup

Preparation Time: 10 minutes
Cooking Time: 6 hours
Serve:6

Ingredients:

- 1 lb (about 453g) dried great northern beans, soaked overnight and drained
- 1 tablespoon garlic, minced
- 4 cups vegetable broth
- ½ teaspoon dried sage
- 1 onion, diced
- 2 celery stalks, diced
- 2 cups water
- 3 carrots, diced
- Pepper and salt

Method:

1. Add beans and remaining ingredients into the slow cooker and stir well.
2. Cover and cook on high for 6 hours.
3. Stir well and serve.

Nutritional Value (Amount per Serving):

- Calories: 305
- Fat: 1.8 g
- Carbohydrates: 53.2 g
- Sugar: 4.5 g
- Protein: 20.4 g
- Cholesterol: 0 mg

Green Bean Tomato Soup

Preparation Time: 10 minutes
Cooking Time: 6 hours
Serve:8

Ingredients:

- 1 lb (about 453g) fresh green beans, cut into 1-inch pieces
- 3 cups fresh tomatoes, diced
- 6 cups chicken stock
- 1 cup carrots, chopped
- 1 cup onions, chopped
- 1 teaspoon basil, dried
- 1 garlic clove, minced
- Pepper and salt

Method:

1. Add green beans and remaining ingredients into the slow cooker and stir well.
2. Cover and cook on low for 6 hours.
3. Stir well and serve.

Nutritional Value (Amount per Serving):

- Calories: 49
- Fat: 0.6 g
- Carbohydrates: 10.1 g
- Sugar: 4.4 g
- Protein: 2.4 g
- Cholesterol: 0 mg

Asian Chicken Soup

Preparation Time: 10 minutes
Cooking Time: 3 hours
Serve:4

Ingredients:

- 1 lb (about 453g) chicken breast, boneless, cooked and chopped
- 14 ounce (about 396g) coconut milk
- 2 tablespoons basil, chopped
- 1 tablespoon garlic powder
- 1 tablespoon ginger root
- 1 tablespoon curry paste
- 2 teaspoon thyme
- 4 cups chicken stock
- 1 cup jasmine rice
- Pepper and salt

Method:

1. Add chicken and remaining ingredients into the slow cooker and stir well.
2. Cover and cook on low for 3 hours.
3. Stir well and serve.

Nutritional Value (Amount per Serving):

- Calories: 562
- Fat: 29.3 g
- Carbohydrates: 45.4 g
- Sugar: 4.6 g
- Protein: 30.6 g
- Cholesterol: 73 mg

Mix Veggie Soup

Preparation Time: 10 minutes
Cooking Time: 8 hours
Serve:2

Ingredients:

- ¼ cup can tomatoes, diced
- ¼ teaspoon white pepper
- 1 teaspoon celery flakes
- 2 cup vegetable stock
- 1 garlic clove, minced
- 1 tablespoon fresh dill
- 1 celery stalk, diced
- 1 small carrot, diced
- ¼ cup celery cubed
- 1 parsnip, diced
- 1 shallot, minced
- ⅛ teaspoon salt

Method:

1. Add parsnip and remaining ingredients into the slow cooker and stir well.
2. Cover and cook on low for 8 hours.
3. Stir well and serve.

Nutritional Value (Amount per Serving):

- Calories: 102
- Fat: 0.6 g
- Carbohydrates: 23 g
- Sugar: 8.2 g
- Protein: 2.9 g
- Cholesterol: 0 mg

Tomato Green Beans Barley Soup

Preparation Time: 10 minutes
Cooking Time: 4 hours
Serve:2

Ingredients:

- 7 ounces (about 198g) can green beans, cut into pieces
- 12 ounce (about 340g) chicken broth
- 1½ cups crushed tomatoes

- ¼ cup barley, uncooked
- ¼ cup ham, chopped
- Pepper and salt

Method:

1. Add beans, ham, tomatoes, barley, broth, pepper, and salt into the slow cooker and stir well.
2. Cover and cook on low for 4 hours.

Nutritional Value (Amount per Serving):

- Calories: 281
- Fat: 3 g
- Carbohydrates: 47.2 g
- Sugar: 18.2 g
- Protein: 17.1 g
- Cholesterol: 10 mg

Curried Cauliflower Soup

Preparation Time: 10 minutes
Cooking Time: 6 hours
Serve:2

Ingredients:

- ½ lb (about 226g) cauliflower florets
- 1½ teaspoon curry powder
- 1 garlic clove, minced
- 1¼ cup vegetable stock
- ½ onion, minced
- ⅛ teaspoon cumin

Method:

1. Add cauliflower florets and remaining ingredients into the slow cooker and stir well.
2. Cover and cook on low for 6 hours.
3. Puree the soup using an immersion blender until smooth.

Nutritional Value (Amount per Serving):

- Calories: 51
- Fat: 0.5 g
- Carbohydrates: 10.6 g
- Sugar: 4.4 g
- Protein: 3.1 g
- Cholesterol: 0 mg

Mexican Chicken Soup

Preparation Time: 10 minutes
Cooking Time: 4 hours
Serve:2

Ingredients:

- 1 chicken breast, cooked and shredded
- 8 ounce (about 226g) chunky salsa
- 16 ounces (about 453g) vegetable broth
- 7 ounce (about 198g) can black beans
- 1 packet of taco seasoning
- ½ cup frozen peas
- ½ cup frozen corn

Method:

1. Add chicken, salsa, broth, taco seasoning, peas, corn, and black beans into the slow cooker and stir well.
2. Cover and cook on low for 4 hours.
3. Stir well and serve.

Nutritional Value (Amount per Serving):

- Calories: 288
- Fat: 3.9 g
- Carbohydrates: 38.5 g
- Sugar: 8 g
- Protein: 26.9 g
- Cholesterol: 36 mg

Jalapeno Pork Soup

Preparation Time: 10 minutes
Cooking Time: 8 hours
Serve:8

Ingredients:

- 1 lb (about 453g) pork loin
- 1½ teaspoon chili powder
- 1 jalapeno pepper, minced
- 2 teaspoons fresh lime juice
- 1½ teaspoon garlic powder
- 1½ teaspoon onion powder
- 1 cup onion, chopped
- 3 tomatoes, chopped
- 8 cups chicken stock
- 1½ teaspoon cumin

Method:

1. Place meat into the slow cooker.
2. Pour the remaining ingredients over the meat.
3. Cover and cook on low for 8 hours.
4. Shred the meat using a fork and stir well.

Nutritional Value (Amount per Serving):

- Calories: 152
- Fat: 7.8 g
- Carbohydrates: 5.4 g
- Sugar: 2.8 g
- Protein: 15.2 g
- Cholesterol: 40 mg

Flavorful Lamb Stew

Preparation Time: 10 minutes
Cooking Time: 6 hours
Serve:6

Ingredients:

- 3 lb (about 1360g) lamb shoulder, cut into pieces
- 28 ounces (about 793g) tomatoes, diced

- 2 onions, diced
- 4 garlic cloves, chopped
- 2 cups white wine
- 4 cups chicken broth
- 1 bay leaf
- ½ Tsp thyme, dried
- 1 teaspoon fresh thyme
- 1 teaspoon oregano, dried
- Pepper and salt

Method:

1. Add meat pieces and remaining ingredients into the slow cooker and stir well.
2. Cover and cook on low for 6 hours.
3. Stir well and serve.

Nutritional Value (Amount per Serving):

- Calories: 556
- Fat: 17.9 g
- Carbohydrates: 12.4 g
- Sugar: 6.1 g
- Protein: 68.7 g
- Cholesterol: 204 mg

Green Bean Tomato Soup

Preparation Time: 10 minutes
Cooking Time: 6 hours
Serve:8

Ingredients:

- 1 lb (about 453g) fresh green beans, cut into 1-inch pieces
- 3 cups fresh tomatoes, diced
- 1 cup carrots, chopped
- 1 cup onions, chopped
- ¼ teaspoon black pepper
- 1 teaspoon basil, dried

- 1 garlic clove, minced
- 6 cups chicken broth
- ½ teaspoon salt

Method:

1. Add green beans and remaining ingredients into the slow cooker and stir well.
2. Cover and cook on low for 6 hours.
3. Stir well and serve.

Nutritional Value (Amount per Serving):

- Calories: 71
- Fat: 1.3 g
- Carbohydrates: 10.2 g
- Sugar: 4.4 g
- Protein: 5.6 g
- Cholesterol: 0 mg

Creamy Carrot Soup

Preparation Time: 10 minutes
Cooking Time: 3 hours
Serve:4

Ingredients:

- 1 tablespoon ginger, chopped
- 1 teaspoon smoked paprika
- 6 carrots, chopped
- 1 cup coconut milk
- 1 garlic clove
- ⅓ cup water
- 1 teaspoon salt

Method:

1. Add carrots and remaining ingredients into the slow cooker and stir well.
2. Cover and cook on low for 3 hours.

3. Puree the soup using a blender until smooth.
4. Stir well and serve warm.

Nutritional Value (Amount per Serving):

- Calories: 183
- Fat: 14.5 g
- Carbohydrates: 13.8 g
- Sugar: 6.6 g
- Protein: 2.4 g
- Cholesterol: 0 mg

Chicken Cheese Soup

Preparation Time: 10 minutes
Cooking Time: 4 hours
Serve:6

Ingredients:

- 1½ lb (about 680g) chicken, boneless and cut into pieces
- 8 ounces (about 226g) pepper jack cheese, shredded
- 15-ounce (about 425g) chunky salsa
- 15-ounce (about 425g) chicken stock

Method:

1. Place chicken into the slow cooker.
2. Pour the remaining ingredients over the chicken.
3. Cover and cook on high for 4 hours.
4. Shred the chicken using a fork.
5. Stir well and serve.

Nutritional Value (Amount per Serving):

- Calories: 342
- Fat: 15.9 g
- Carbohydrates: 4.7 g
- Sugar: 2.4 g
- Protein: 43.6 g
- Cholesterol: 128 mg

Spinach Bean Soup

Preparation Time: 10 minutes
Cooking Time: 6 hours
Serve:6

Ingredients:

- 14 ounces (about 396g) can of white beans, rinsed and drained
- 14-ounce (about 396g) can of tomato puree
- 8 cups fresh spinach, chopped
- 1 teaspoon dried basil, crushed
- 1 teaspoon garlic, minced
- ½ cup onion, chopped
- ½ cup brown rice
- 5 ½ cups vegetable broth
- Pepper and salt

Method:

1. Add beans, basil, garlic, onion, rice, tomato puree, broth, pepper, and salt into the slow cooker and mix well.
2. Cover and cook on low for 6 hours.
3. Add spinach and stir until spinach is wilted.

Nutritional Value (Amount per Serving):

- Calories: 197
- Fat: 2.2 g
- Carbohydrates: 35.4 g
- Sugar: 4.6 g
- Protein: 12.8 g
- Cholesterol: 0 mg

Broccoli Spinach Soup

Preparation Time: 10 minutes
Cooking Time: 4 hours 30 minutes
Serve:6

- 5 ounces (about 141g) baby spinach
- 4½ cups vegetable broth
- 3 garlic cloves, minced
- 2½ cups broccoli florets
- 1 cup onion, chopped
- ½ teaspoon pepper
- 1½ teaspoon salt

Method:

1. Add broccoli, onion, broth, garlic, pepper, and salt into the slow cooker and stir well.
2. Cover and cook on high for 4 hours.
3. Add spinach and cook for 30 minutes more.
4. Puree the soup using a blender until smooth.

Nutritional Value (Amount per Serving):

- Calories: 58
- Fat: 1.3 g
- Carbohydrates: 6.5 g
- Sugar: 2.1 g
- Protein: 5.7 g
- Cholesterol: 0 mg

Chicken Vegetable Soup

Preparation Time: 10 minutes
Cooking Time: 3 hours 30 minutes
Serve:4

Ingredients:

- ½ lb (about 226g) chicken breasts, diced
- 8 ounce (about 226g) mushrooms, sliced
- 2 celery stalks, chopped
- 4 cups chicken broth
- 4 green onions, diced

- ½ teaspoon pepper
- 2 carrots, chopped
- 1 onion, chopped
- 1 teaspoon salt
- 2 cups water

Method:

1. Add chicken and remaining ingredients into the slow cooker and stir well.
2. Cover and cook on high for 3 hours.
3. Add green onions and mushrooms and stir well.
4. Cover again and cook for 30 minutes more.
5. Stir well and serve.

Nutritional Value (Amount per Serving):

- Calories: 189
- Fat: 5.8 g
- Carbohydrates: 9.9 g
- Sugar: 4.8 g
- Protein: 23.9 g
- Cholesterol: 50 mg

Healthy Asparagus Soup

Preparation Time: 10 minutes
Cooking Time: 4 hours
Serve:4

Ingredients:

- 1 lb (about 453g) asparagus, trimmed and chopped
- 2 cups chicken broth
- 2 tablespoons olive oil
- ½ cup onion, chopped
- ¼ teaspoon pepper
- ½ teaspoon salt

Method:

1. Add asparagus and remaining ingredients into the slow cooker and stir well.
2. Cover and cook on high for 4 hours.
3. Puree the soup using a blender until smooth.
4. Stir well and serve.

Nutritional Value (Amount per Serving):

- Calories: 108
- Fat: 7.8 g
- Carbohydrates: 6.3 g
- Sugar: 3.1 g
- Protein: 5.1 g
- Cholesterol: 0 mg

White Chicken Chili

Preparation Time: 10 minutes
Cooking Time: 8 hours
Serve:8

Ingredients:

- 30 ounces (about 850g) can of great northern beans, drained and rinsed
- 4 chicken breasts, skinless and boneless
- 8 ounce (about 226g) can green chilies, chopped
- 2 garlic cloves, minced
- 1 small onion, chopped
- 1 teaspoon dried oregano
- 1 teaspoon ground cumin
- 1 tablespoon chili powder
- 1 jalapeno pepper, minced
- 6 cups chicken broth

Method:

1. Place chicken into the slow cooker.
2. Pour the remaining ingredients over the chicken and stir well.
3. Cover and cook on low for 8 hours.

4. Shred the chicken using a fork.
5. Stir well and serve.

Nutritional Value (Amount per Serving):

- Calories: 304
- Fat: 7.2 g
- Carbohydrates: 26.3 g
- Sugar: 1.1 g
- Protein: 33.2 g
- Cholesterol: 65 mg

Sweet Potato Soup

Preparation Time: 10 minutes
Cooking Time: 4 hours
Serve:4

Ingredients:

- 2 lb (about 907g) sweet potatoes, peeled and chopped
- 4 cups vegetable broth
- 4 leeks, sliced
- 1 tablespoon olive oil
- ½ teaspoon thyme
- ¼ teaspoon pepper
- 1½ teaspoon garlic salt

Method:

1. Add sweet potatoes and remaining ingredients into the slow cooker and stir well.
2. Cover and cook on low for 4 hours.
3. Puree the soup using a blender until smooth.

Nutritional Value (Amount per Serving):

- Calories: 394
- Fat: 5.6 g
- Carbohydrates: 77.7 g
- Sugar: 5.6 g
- Protein: 9.9 g
- Cholesterol: 0 mg

Easy Shrimp Soup

Preparation Time: 10 minutes
Cooking Time: 2 hours 10 minutes
Serve:4

Ingredients:

- 64 ounces (about 1814g) chicken stock
- ½ green bell pepper, sliced
- 1 tablespoon old bay seasoning
- 1 lb (about 453g) shrimp
- ½ red bell pepper, sliced
- 1 onion, sliced

Method:

1. Add all ingredients except shrimp into the slow cooker and stir well.
2. Cover and cook on low for 2 hours.
3. Add shrimp and cook for 10 minutes more.
4. Stir well and serve.

Nutritional Value (Amount per Serving):

- Calories: 173
- Fat: 3.1 g
- Carbohydrates: 7.9 g
- Sugar: 4 g
- Protein: 27.7 g
- Cholesterol: 239 mg

Red Lentil Soup

Preparation Time: 10 minutes
Cooking Time: 5 hours
Serve:6

Ingredients:

- 2 cups dried red lentils, rinsed
- 2½ tablespoons lemon juice
- 1 tablespoon garlic, minced
- 1 small onion, diced
- 3 carrots, peel and dice
- ½ tablespoon dried herbs
- 6 cups chicken stock
- 2 tablespoons olive oil
- Pepper and salt

Method:

1. Heat olive oil in a pan over medium heat.
2. Add garlic, carrots, and onion, and sauté for 5 minutes.
3. Season with pepper and salt.
4. Add sautéed onion and carrot mixture into the slow cooker.
5. Add remaining ingredients and stir well.
6. Cover and cook on low for 5 hours.
7. Stir well and serve.

Nutritional Value (Amount per Serving):

- Calories: 297
- Fat: 6 g
- Carbohydrates: 43.9 g
- Sugar: 4.1 g
- Protein: 17.7 g
- Cholesterol: 0 mg

Beef Okra Stew

Preparation Time: 10 minutes
Cooking Time: 4 hours
Serve:2

Ingredients:

- 1 lb (about 453g) beef, diced
- 1 cup fresh okra, chopped
- 2 garlic cloves, crushed

- 1 large onion, chopped
- 1 tablespoon olive oil
- 2 cups vegetable stock
- ¼ teaspoon cinnamon
- ½ teaspoon pepper
- 1 teaspoon cumin
- Salt

Method:

1. Heat olive oil in a pan over medium heat.
2. Add meat and cook from all sides until brown.
3. Transfer the meat into the slow cooker.
4. Add remaining ingredients and stir well.
5. Cover and cook on low for 4 hours.

Nutritional Value (Amount per Serving):

- Calories: 548
- Fat: 21.7 g
- Carbohydrates: 13.7 g
- Sugar: 4.7 g
- Protein: 71.5 g
- Cholesterol: 203 mg

Chicken Veggie Stew

Preparation Time: 10 minutes
Cooking Time: 6 hours 5 minutes
Serve:6

Ingredients:

- 1 lb (about 453g) chicken breasts, boneless
- 3 ½ cups vegetable broth
- 2 cups butternut squash, cubed
- 1½ tablespoon sage, minced
- 1 teaspoon garlic powder
- 1 tablespoon olive oil
- 1 cup carrots, chopped

- 1 onion, chopped
- Pepper and salt

Method:

1. Heat oil in a pan over medium heat.
2. Add onion and saute for 5 minutes.
3. Transfer sauteed onion into the slow cooker along with the remaining ingredients and stir well.
4. Cover and cook on low for 6 hours.
5. Shred chicken using a fork.
6. Stir well and serve.

Nutritional Value (Amount per Serving):

- Calories: 225
- Fat: 8.9 g
- Carbohydrates: 10.2 g
- Sugar: 3.2 g
- Protein: 25.7 g
- Cholesterol: 67 mg

Chapter 9: Appetizers and Sauces

Spaghetti Sauce

Preparation Time: 10 minutes
Cooking Time: 6 hours
Serve:10

Ingredients:

- 42 ounces (about 1190g) can tomatoes, diced
- 18 ounces (about 226g) can of tomato paste
- ⅛ teaspoon sugar
- 1 tablespoon dried parsley
- 2 bay leaves
- 1 teaspoon Italian seasoning
- ½ teaspoon dried thyme
- ½ teaspoon garlic powder
- ½ teaspoon dried oregano
- 2 cups water
- 1 tablespoon butter
- 3 garlic cloves, chopped
- 1 small onion, diced
- ¼ teaspoon salt

Method:

1. Add tomatoes and remaining ingredients into the slow cooker and stir well.
2. Cover and cook on low for 6 hours.
3. Puree the sauce using an immersion blender until smooth.

Nutritional Value (Amount per Serving):

- Calories: 85
- Fat: 1.6 g
- Carbohydrates: 17.1 g
- Sugar: 10.7 g
- Protein: 3.5 g
- Cholesterol: 3 mg

Cinnamon Applesauce

Preparation Time: 10 minutes
Cooking Time: 8 hours
Serve:10

Ingredients:

- 5 lb (about 2267g) apples, peeled, cored and chopped
- 1 tablespoon cinnamon
- ½ cup brown sugar
- ¾ cup sugar

Method:

1. Add apples, cinnamon, brown sugar, and sugar into the slow cooker and stir well.
2. Cover and cook on low for 8 hours.
3. Puree the sauce using an immersion blender until smooth.

Nutritional Value (Amount per Serving):

- Calories: 143
- Fat: 0.2 g
- Carbohydrates: 38.1 g
- Sugar: 33.6 g
- Protein: 0.3 g
- Cholesterol: 0 mg

Marinara Sauce

Preparation Time: 10 minutes
Cooking Time: 8 hours
Serve:6

Ingredients:

- 24-ounce (about 680g) crushed tomatoes
- 6 ounce (about 170g) tomato paste
- 6 ounces (about 170g) of water

- 1 teaspoon dried oregano
- 1 teaspoon dried parsley
- 2 teaspoons dried basil
- 1 onion, chopped
- 1 tablespoon olive oil
- 1 carrot, chopped
- ½ teaspoon salt

Method:

1. Add crushed tomatoes and remaining ingredients into the slow cooker and stir well.
2. Cover and cook on low for 8 hours.
3. Puree the sauce using an immersion blender until smooth.

Nutritional Value (Amount per Serving):

- Calories: 101
- Fat: 2.5 g
- Carbohydrates: 17.3 g
- Sugar: 11.1 g
- Protein: 4.3 g
- Cholesterol: 0 mg

Enchilada Dip

Preparation Time: 10 minutes
Cooking Time: 2 hours
Serve:8

Ingredients:

- 4 ounce (about 113g) cream cheese, cut into pieces
- 4 ounce (about 113g) green chilies, diced
- 1 lb (about 453g) ground meat, browned
- 2 cups cheddar cheese, shredded
- 1 tablespoon taco seasoning
- 1 tablespoon olive oil
- 2 cups enchilada sauce

Method:

1. Add meat, oil, cream cheese, chilies, taco seasoning, sauce, and cheese into the slow cooker and stir well.

2. Cover and cook on high for 2 hours.
3. Stir well and serve.

Nutritional Value (Amount per Serving):

- Calories: 361
- Fat: 21.6 g
- Carbohydrates: 17.1 g
- Sugar: 6.1 g
- Protein: 27.3 g
- Cholesterol: 96 mg

Chicken Dip

Preparation Time: 10 minutes
Cooking Time: 4 hours
Serve:16

Ingredients:

- 4 cups chicken breast, cooked and shredded
- 1½ cups cheddar cheese, shredded
- 8 ounce (about 226g) cream cheese
- 1 cup ranch dressing
- ¾ cup buffalo sauce

Method:

1. Add cooked chicken and remaining ingredients into the slow cooker and stir well.
2. Cover and cook on low for 4 hours.
3. Stir well and serve.

Nutritional Value (Amount per Serving):

- Calories: 129
- Fat: 9.2 g
- Carbohydrates: 1.4 g
- Sugar: 0.5 g
- Protein: 9.8 g
- Cholesterol: 45 mg

Queso Dip

Preparation Time: 10 minutes
Cooking Time: 1 hour
Serve:10

Ingredients:

- 30 ounces (about 850g) no bean chili
- 32 ounces (about 907g) of Velveeta cheese
- ½ teaspoon cayenne
- 2 tablespoons cumin
- 2 tablespoon paprika
- 3 tablespoons chili powder
- 6 tablespoons lime juice
- 2 cups milk

Method:

1. Add cheese and remaining ingredients into the slow cooker and stir well.
2. Cover and cook on high for 1 hour.
3. Stir well and serve.

Nutritional Value (Amount per Serving):

- Calories: 384
- Fat: 23.4 g
- Carbohydrates: 26.8 g
- Sugar: 11.9 g
- Protein: 23.6 g
- Cholesterol: 76 mg

Cranberry Sauce

Preparation Time: 10 minutes
Cooking Time: 3 hours
Serve:8

Ingredients:

- 12 ounce (about 340g) frozen cranberries
- 1 orange, seedless, peeled and sectioned
- 1 cinnamon stick
- 2 bay leaves
- ⅔ cup sugar

Method:

1. Add cranberries, cinnamon sticks, bay leaves, orange, and sugar into the slow cooker and stir well.
2. Cover and cook on high for 3 hours.
3. Stir well and serve.

Nutritional Value (Amount per Serving):

- Calories: 94
- Fat: 0 g
- Carbohydrates: 24.7 g
- Sugar: 23 g
- Protein: 0.2 g
- Cholesterol: 0 mg

Creamy Reuben Dip

Preparation Time: 10 minutes
Cooking Time: 2 hours 30 minutes
Serve:10

Ingredients:

- 8 ounces (about 226g) cream cheese, softened
- 14-ounce (about 396g) can sauerkraut, squeezed
- ½ lb (about 226g) deli corned beef, sliced
- 1½ cups Swiss cheese, shredded
- ½ teaspoon Worcestershire sauce
- 1 tablespoon milk
- ⅓ cup mayonnaise

Method:

1. Add cream cheese and remaining ingredients into the slow cooker and stir well.
2. Cover and cook on low for 2½ hours.
3. Stir well and serve.

Nutritional Value (Amount per Serving):

- Calories: 218
- Fat: 17.4 g
- Carbohydrates: 5.5 g
- Sugar: 1.9 g
- Protein: 10.7 g
- Cholesterol: 55 mg

Chili Cheese Dip

Preparation Time: 10 minutes
Cooking Time: 2 hours
Serve:12

Ingredients:

- 30-ounce (about 850g) can of chili con carne without beans
- 8 ounce (about 226g) can green chilies, chopped
- 32 ounce (about 907g) Velveeta cheese, cubed

Method:

1. Add cheese, green chilies, and chili con carne into the slow cooker and mix well.
2. Cover and cook on low for 2 hours.
3. Stir well and serve.

Nutritional Value (Amount per Serving):

- Calories: 297
- Fat: 18.4 g
- Carbohydrates: 12.2 g
- Sugar: 5.4 g
- Protein: 24.7 g
- Cholesterol: 61 mg

Artichoke Spinach Dip

Preparation Time: 10 minutes
Cooking Time: 2 hours
Serve:6

Ingredients:

- 8 ounces (about 226g) cream cheese, cut into cubes
- 14 ounces (about 396g) can artichoke hearts, chopped
- 10 ounce (about 283g) spinach, chopped
- ½ cup parmesan cheese, shredded
- 1 cup mozzarella cheese, shredded
- 4 garlic cloves, minced
- 1 cup sour cream
- Pepper and salt

Method:

1. Add spinach and remaining ingredients into the slow cooker and stir well.
2. Cover and cook on low for 2 hours.
3. Stir well and serve.

Nutritional Value (Amount per Serving):

- Calories: 285
- Fat: 23.8 g
- Carbohydrates: 8.8 g
- Sugar: 0.9 g
- Protein: 10.4 g
- Cholesterol: 66 mg

Made in the USA
Middletown, DE
07 September 2023

38101116R00064